ALL ]

MW01118732

CAUTION: Professionals and amateurs are hereby warned that this play is subject to royalty. It is fully protected by Original Works Publishing, and the copyright laws of the United States. All rights, including professional, amateur, motion pictures, recitation, lecturing, public reading, radio broadcasting, television, and the rights of translation into foreign languages are strictly reserved.

The performance rights to this play are controlled by Original Works Publishing and royalty arrangements and licenses must be secured well in advance of presentation. PLEASE NOTE that amateur royalty fees are set upon application in accordance with your producing circumstances. When applying for a royalty quotation and license please give us the number of performances intended, dates of production, your seating capacity and admission fee. Royalties are payable with negotiation from Original Works Publishing.

Royalty of the required amount must be paid whether the play is presented for charity or gain and whether or not admission is charged. Particular emphasis is laid on the question of amateur or professional readings, permission and terms for which must be secured from Original Works Publishing through direct contact.

Copying from this book in whole or in part is strictly forbidden by law, and the right of performance is not transferable.

Whenever the play is produced the following notice must appear on all programs, printing, and advertising for the play:
**"Produced by special arrangement with**
**Original Works Publishing."**
www.originalworksonline.com
Due authorship credit must be given on all programs, printing and advertising for the play.

# More Great Plays Available From Original Works Publishing

## THE ARCTIC CIRCLE
### by Samantha Macher

3 Males, 2 Females

**Synopsis:** A Brechtian comedy about a woman in a troubled marriage who travels through time, space and Sweden to reexamine her past relationships for solutions to her newly found troubles. Unable to get the clear answers she needs, she must look inside herself to find what she is looking for.

## NURTURE
### by Johnna Adams

1 Male, 1 Female

**Synopsis**: Doug and Cheryl are horrible single parents drawn together by their equally horrible daughters. The star-crossed parental units journey from first meeting to first date, to first time, to first joint parent-teacher meeting, to proposal and more. They attempt to form a modern nuclear family while living in perpetual fear of the fruit of their loins and someone abducting young girls in their town.

# MITZI'S ABORTION

## (A Saint's Guide to Late-Term Politics and Medicine in America)

By
Elizabeth Heffron

The World Premiere of *Mitzi's Abortion* was presented by ACT Theatre, July 2006. It was directed by Kurt Beattie. Sets were designed by Narelle Sissons, costumes by Sarah Nash Gates, lights by Chris Reay, sound by Dominic Cody Kramers, and the stage manager was JR Welden. The cast was as follows:

| | |
|---|---|
| MITZI | *Sharia Pierce* |
| CHUCK,<br>THE EXPERT,<br>SERGEI | *Sean Cook* |
| VERA | *Kit Harris* |
| AQUINAS,<br>TIM,<br>THE GENETICIST | *Eric Ray Anderson* |
| RECKLESS MARY,<br>SHEILA LUFFINGTON | *Leslie Law* |
| NITA,<br>NURSE | *Shelley Reynolds* |
| RUDOLFO,<br>DR. BLOCK,<br>UNCLE TUB | *Richard Ziman* |

# CAST OF CHARACTERS

**MITZI**       22

**CHUCK**       24
     *also plays*       THE EXPERT
                         SERGEI, an ultrasound technician

**VERA**       Mitzi's Mom, early 50s

**RUDOLFO**       Mitzi's Stepdad, 50s
     *also plays*       DR. BLOCK, an OB/GYN
                         UNCLE TUB, Vera's brother, late 50's

**THOMAS AQUINAS**
                         13th-century Catholic Saint, late 30-40s
     *also plays*       TIM, friend of Mitzi and Nita
                         A GENETICIST

**NITA**       Mitzi's friend, 30's
     *also plays*       NURSE

**RECKLESS MARY** 17th-century Charred Midwife, 30-50s
     *also plays*       SHEILA LUFFINGTON,
                         an insurance worker

## TIME
Winter, 2002, through Summer, 2003.

## PLACE
Burien, Washington, and other Seattle locations.

PLEASE NOTE: The play is intended to run without an intermission. All scenes changes should be brisk and minimal. Although some of the characters may sound harsh or funny, they should not be played as caricatures. They are all human beings just doing the best they can.

# MITZI'S ABORTION

*(Lights up on Saint Thomas Aquinas, all 350 pounds of him, swathed in Dominican robes. He lays sprawled over a black leather, self-massaging chair from the Sharper Image.)*

THOMAS AQUINAS: *(his voice quivers from the effect of the vibrating chair)* Ahhhhhhhh. Hallelujah. Now this… is sin. *(he shifts his weight luxuriously)* 4 'human touch' rollers deviously replicating professional massage techniques… pummeling my backside like a band of Swedish chiropractors. If the Sharper Image had existed in 1272, I would never have finished my opus, the *Summa Theologica*. Not in a million years. *(he finds the control panel, starts to punch buttons)* My God! How does one handle this panoply of consumer temptations, shaking their electric doodads before you like digital strippers? Oh! Not to mention Anderson Cooper! I know he's a Vanderbilt, but I think I'm in love! There he is, every evening at 10… dishing out the most heinous atrocities with such audacious panache! Such arousing directness… makes you just want to kiss the screen.

*(Hitting the 'off' button, rising from the chair, getting down to business.)*

AQUINAS: But, we're not here to ogle Anderson Cooper. No we are not. We're here to begin a play about a late-term abortion. Downer subject, don't you think? Moist and slightly repellent, like most female issues. The Church has had the better part of 2,000 years to come to terms with that sex, and just when you think you've got a handle on them, they show up to the party attached to the Evil Three… (continued)

7

AQUINAS (Cont'd): Ta-ta's, Tush, and that bloody bowl of infinite contention, the Uterus. There they are, walking around, drinking martinis, laughing in our faces, like this... *(he demonstrates a female giggle)* "A-ha-ha-ha-ha-ha!" And once again, we are forced to consider the nature of those biological items. The outlandish, conceptual function they advertise like cheap underwear. It is so distastefully tawdry to know that all human life — even Anderson Cooper's — begins in just such a dark and festering cavern. If I weren't such a saint, it would really grate on the old ego. Imagine... Andy Cooper in utero! It's pornographic really. But. What can one do? God is great, and yet he seems to extract a rather carnal pleasure by working in such mysterious ways. Anyway, you didn't come here to be lectured by an old Catholic fuddy-duddy, like Thomas Aquinas, no-no, you came to meet Mitzi. May Yahweh be with you...

*(Lights down on Aquinas and up center stage. Mitzi sits on a toilet. Chuck, in a U.S. Army uniform, stands patiently nearby.)*

MITZI: I mean it's not like I'm never gonna make it back to Seattle U, right Chuck? I can keep working at Subway and saving up and studying and stuff. Kids nap, and there's day care. And my Esperanto group, I'm not gonna stop doing Esperanto.

CHUCK: You don't have to stop doing Esperanto. Here.

*(Chuck hands Mitzi a pregnancy stick. She takes it and sticks it under her, between her legs.)*

MITZI: How long?

CHUCK:  Uhhh, *(reading the box)* Mid-stream.  5 to 10 seconds.

MITZI:  *(waiting for pee)*  So.  Anyway.  It's good to be clear, right?

CHUCK:  Yeah.  Are you peeing?

MITZI:  Shhhh…

CHUCK:  What?

MITZI:  Don't talk about it.

CHUCK:  Why not?

MITZI:  If you talk about it, I can't do it, you know?  Shuts me right down.

CHUCK:  You mean, like, with sex.

MITZI:  Yeah.  Exactly.

*(Chuck considers this.)*

CHUCK:  Maybe we should get married.

MITZI:  Married?  Why?

CHUCK:  Insurance.  You have insurance?

MITZI:  I don't know.  I probably checked 'no' on that box.

CHUCK: Yeah, that's what I thought. That's why it's good I'm in the Army. I got good insurance. It'll cover a baby and stuff, but we'd have to –

MITZI: Whoa, hang on. Here it comes... *(he moves closer)* No, not so close. Don't look at me. Turn around, okay?

CHUCK: Sure.

*(Chuck turns around. Mitzi concentrates on the stick.)*

MITZI: Okay, now start counting.

CHUCK: Uh. One. Two. Three. Four. Five... *(turning back)* Okay stop.

MITZI: Stop? I can't stop. Don't look, turn, turn. This is like really personal...

*(She finishes, wipes, flushes, pulls up her pants.)*

MITZI: Okay.

*(Chuck turns back around. Mitzi hands him the stick.)*

MITZI: So... is there a blue dot?

*(He holds it slight away, tries to scrutinize it.)*

MITZI: Maybe we shouldn't try for this now, you know? I mean I'm still paying off that DVD player, and we got a lot going on, with you going to the Middle East and everything...

CHUCK:  There's a blue dot.

MITZI:  There is?  No way!  It's supposed to take a couple of months or something.

CHUCK:  Blue dot.  Right there.

MITZI:  Lemme see.

CHUCK:  Fuck, I'm good!

MITZI:  Maybe it's… like, a negative, you know?  Maybe it means --

CHUCK:  Nope, it means I got the juice, baby!  Oh yeah!

MIZI:  Lemme see the box.

CHUCK:  Sperm-o-matic!

*(She reads the box, concedes he's right.)*

MITZI:  Yeah… you're good.

CHUCK:  Fuckin' One-Shot-Sam, that's me!  Gimme-gimme, baby.

*(Chuck pulls her to him, they kiss.)*

CHUCK:  Damn, I oughta sell my squirt.  One of those sperm banks.  You hungry?  Let's go out!

*(The news is sinking in for Mitzi.)*

MITZI:  Pregnant.  Wow…

CHUCK: How 'bout eggs? Let's hit Huckleberry's.

MITZI: Hey Chuck...

CHUCK: You seen my Nikes?

MITZI: Chuck, what if... I mean, not that I'm saying this but, what if... right now... isn't exactly --

CHUCK: It's what we want. We talked about it, remember? You're 22 and I'm 24.

MITZI: But, I mean, what if it's like what we thought we wanted on the surface, you know? Like a coat of paint or something? But what if the house isn't ready to be lived in yet? You know?

CHUCK: You're scared. Afraid it's gonna change your life.

MITZI: Yeah.

CHUCK: C'mon, let's go eat.

MITZI: And what about my Beginning Catholicism Forum, and my Great Books Group, and that Copier Repair class? I mean, maybe I haven't completely funneled my future down yet.

CHUCK: You can keep funneling, baby. Do your book group. You can read and still have a kid. You can copy, talk Esperanto, all-a-that. They're simpatico.

MITZI: I don't know...

CHUCK: Wear your pink sweater. You look like a momma in pink.

*(Mitzi slowly puts on her pink sweater, as Chuck disappears. She checks to make sure that nobody's looking. She hits herself in the stomach. She hits herself in the stomach several times. She throws herself to the ground, gets up, and throws herself to the ground again.*

*During the above, lights go up on a charred midwife, Reckless Mary. She leans against a rather authentic-looking stake. Her scorched appearance should indicate she's been the victim of a witch-hunt. Mitzi does not see her.)*

MARY: Aye, leap, sister. Leap off a fekkin cliff if it helps. Bound around like a wild boar 'till ye limbs go slack. Ets one method, 'course if ye kin climb atop that boar and ride 'til it throws ya, that's even better. Hippocrates himself'd tellya the same. But there be other ways too. Might I commend ya ta rub down your vagina with wine, then insert a wad comprised of two parts grated pomegranate peel and one part oak galls. Some would add to that a bit of stinkin' iris, but I say that's best chewed and swallowed.

*(MITZI, exhausted, sits slumped on the ground.)*

MARY: You just listen to me, sister. I've been midwife to both life and death. They call me 'Reckless Mary' for I did wantonly proclaim my healing arts and burned fer it. They don't like cunning, the prick-ed ones. They don't like skirts what don't produce neither, so you'd best not mention your ponderings, specially to the one that did the prickin'…

13

*(MITZI pulls herself together and gets up, adjusting her clothes. As she does, VERA approaches, wiping down a dish.)*

VERA: Knocked up, huh? How long?

MITZI: Couple weeks. Maybe… four or five. Eight.

VERA: Took your time telling us.

MITZI: We wanted, you know… to be sure.

VERA: Uh-huh.

MITZI: We're getting married tomorrow. Downtown. *(showing Vera her ring)* See? From the Shane Company! Chuck went all out, and we don't have to make any payments until 2005.

VERA: Uh-huh. *(calling downstairs)* Rudolfo! Mitzi's here. You were right. *(to Mitzi)* He had you pegged right away. I said you weren't that short-sighted. You had your plans. You were gonna go back to that college.

MITZI: I'm still going back.

VERA: Uh-huh. *(she yells down for Rudolfo again)* Rudolfo! She's pregnant and getting married!

MITZI: And moving into his apartment next week.

VERA: What's the rush? Hope you got a good feel for this guy.

*(Rudolfo appears with a remote. He hands it to Vera.)*

RUDOLFO:  This ain't the right remote, Vera.

VERA:  I thought it was.

*(Rudolfo hugs Mitzi.)*

RUDOLFO:  Hey baby.

MITZI:  Hey daddy.

RUDOLFO:  *(looking around)*  So where's your man?

MITZI:  Out in the car.  Wanted to break it to you first.

VERA:  Well, you broke it to us.  Bring him in.

MITZI:  *(calling out the door)*  Hey Chuck!  *(BIG WHIS-TLE)  (she waves him in)*

*(Rudolfo and Vera size him up from afar.)*

RUDOLFO:  *(impressed)*  Nice Taurus.

VERA:  *(nervous to meet him)*  I just hope he's not gonna be one of those do-it-yourselfers that camp out right there in the hospital.  That's the most annoying thing I ever heard.  The bozo that got Jeanette's daughter pregnant had a stopwatch, the whole nine yards.  She said when it came Lynelle's time, the guy practically stuffed his arm up her muff and yanked the kid out.  *(re: Chuck)*  What's he getting out of the trunk?

MITZI:  Flowers, for you.

15

VERA: Huh. Yeah, any man who stands there and watches his wife give birth, *that's* a guy who suddenly can't get it up. Ought to be against the law. He keeps his hair nice and short.

MITZI: He's in the army.

VERA: He's got a good stride too. Huh…

*(Chuck comes up, holding flowers.)*

MITZI: Chuck, these are my parents. Vera…

*(Chuck hands Vera the flowers.)*

CHUCK: Mrs. Mendoza…

VERA: Well, aren't you sweet! These are just lovely.

MITZI: And Rudolfo.

*(The two men shake.)*

CHUCK: Mr. Mendoza.

RUDOLFO: Call me Rudolfo. I'm Mitzi's stepdad –

VERA: You're her dad, Rudolfo.

RUDOLFO: I know that Vera, I'm just tryin' to explain things to the man. We had her name changed to Mendoza, uhh… when Vera?

VERA: What?

RUDOLFO:   How old was Mitzi when she became a Mendoza?

VERA:  Had to have been, three.  Three and a half.  'Cuz let's see... she was 6 months when I snuck out of Fresno, and around two, when you and me met at that AA meeting in Federal Way.

RUDOLFO:  That wasn't AA, that was NA.

VERA:  NA?  Rudolfo —

RUDOLFO:   I remember, baby, that was before we switched over to AA.

VERA:  NA, AA, what's the difference?  It was the one at St. Pat's.

RUDOLFO:  That's right.

MITZI:  So --

VERA:   She was a Putzmeier, originally, but boy, was that ever a mistake.

MITZI:  Mom, you don't have to get into all of that.

VERA:  I know I don't.  Whaduya think?  I'm gonna sit here and tell him my whole sad story?

MITZI:  I don't remember my real dad.

VERA:   That's 'cause he OD'd in a Target parking lot, 'bout 8 months after me and Mitz left California. (continued)

VERA (Cont'd): And you know -- not to wish death on anyone -- but it sure as hell was a relief to know that that guy's cratered-up face wasn't gonna pull a 'Heeeere's Johnny!' on me some rainy night down the line. Fact, when I heard from my ex-girlfriend Lucinda, 'bout how he'd passed and all, I swear it felt like I'd just taken the biggest fuckin' *dump* of my life. Such relief, I cannot describe.

*(Short pause.)*

RUDOLFO: So. You're in the infantry, huh? I did two years in the Navy myself.

CHUCK: Yessir.

VERA: And where you from?

CHUCK: Missouri.

VERA: Missouri? What's the religion there?

MITZI: Mom, what do you care about his religion?

VERA: We're talkin' about the future of my grandchild, are we not?

CHUCK: They got pretty much everything in Missouri, lotta Baptist.

VERA: Baptist. That's good. Rudolfo here's training Mitzi to be a step-Catholic. Now, I was raised Four-Square Evangelical myself, although I've been lapsed awhile. In the Four-Square Church, they don't spend a whole lotta time picking things apart. (continued)

18

VERA (Cont'd): What does this mean? What does that mean?' Just give 'em a psalm and they start thumpin'. So where's this apartment of yours?

CHUCK: Lakewood, near the base, block or so off 99.

MITZI: It's really cute! It's gotta garbage disposal.

VERA: *(pulling Chuck towards the kitchen with her)* C'mon in the kitchen. We got tacos.

RUDOLFO: Uhhh... that's quite a haul, Burien to Ft. Lewis.

VERA: *(as she exits with Chuck)* Oh hell Rudolfo, we're down in Fife all the time gettin' parts for the RV.

RUDOLFO: *(has to concede this)* That's true. *(turns to Mitzi, a private moment)* So... you caught yourself a Taurus-man, eh...?

MITZI: *(beat, smiles)* Yeah. I guess I did...

*(Mitzi and Rudolfo follow the other two into the kitchen, as lights rise on an empty podium. The Expert hurries on, he's late, still putting on his shirt and tie, as he begins the lecture.)*

THE EXPERT: Okay! Welcome everybody, to Psych Tuesday. Our case today is a primigravida, 22, named Mitzi. And what we have just witnessed are classic early scenes from a psychological progression of the first trimester. Note Mitzi's marked ambivalence toward her condition. This is quite typical of the first 2 months of pregnancy.           (continued)

19

THE EXPERT (Cont'd): From an evolutionary stand-point, this noncommittal stance is quite advantageous, due to the extremely high rate of spontaneous abortion that occurs during this time frame. Somewhere between 50 to 75% of all fertilized eggs are flushed from the body by week 8. And this figure doesn't include those ejected deliberately. So, obviously, were the female to invest psychologically every time she conceived, she'd be an emotional dish rag by the time she was 30.

*(The Expert's cell phone rings, he answers it.)*

THE EXPERT: Yes? *(holds up a finger to his audience, as if to say this'll just take a minute, turns slightly)* I'm in the middle of a lecture. *(he listens)* Well, which type of bark did they deliver? *(he listens)* But we asked for the shredded... *(listens)* Well, I know but we ordered the shredded. They'll have to take it back. *(listens)* They've got shovels, don't they? They can shovel it all back in the trucks. *(his caller objects)* Jen... Jen. I'm just not into clumps. *(listens)* Yes. Okay.

*(The Expert closes up his phone.)*

THE EXPERT: *(no apology, picking right up)* So. As Klaus and Kennell have outlined in their text, Mitzi will now begin the process of attachment. This emotional change is characterized by passivity, a deepening introversion -- with concurrent loss of interest in external activities -- and most significantly, an overwhelming primary narcissism. In the late first trimester, the female does not yet perceive the fetus as separate from herself, but rather as an extension of her own body.

*(Mitzi appears in her Subway uniform. Her hair's differ-
ent, more done up. As she wipes down the counter, Nita
and Tim approach her station.)*

MITZI:  Welcome to Subway. What'll you have?

NITA:  I'm gonna have your ass.

TIM:  She doesn't get your ass. I get your ass.

MITZI:  Hey Nita, Tim.

NITA:  You missed my birthday party!

MITZI:  I'm sorry –

NITA:  You don't call! You stop coming to Esperanto!

MITZI:  I haven't stopped, I just –– *(switching to Esperanto)* *"Mario diras, ke la kato estas malsana."* (In
English, this means: "Mary says the cat is sick.")

NITA:  Well, *"Paulo skribas al sia patrino"* (Paul is writ-
ing to his mother.)*,* so screw you. I mean, we're like
thinking, what did we fucking do?

MITZI:  I knew you'd be pissed at me.

NITA:  I AM pissed!

TIM:  I'm not that pissed.

NITA:  You're an idiot! You meet the one guy at Game-
Works with his shoes tied. You fuck him, you get
pregnant –

21

TIM: Nita.

NITA: You move IN with him, all in what? Like FOUR months?!

TIM: Nita.

NITA: I mean why didn't you just go to the drugstore and 'Plan B' it? It's easy. I've done it like 3 times and I'm bisexual.

MITZI: I know... but Chuck wants it, and I... kinda want it too.

NITA: You 'kinda want it too'? You're twenty-two, you can't possibly want it. I'm thirty-one, and I don't want it.

TIM: Honey, I got news for you. You may never want it.

MITZI: Look, Nita, you know? I'm just. I'm really sorry.

*(Nita sighs heavily. The Expert finishes up.)*

THE EXPERT: This narcissistic thinking has survival significance for the fetus, as by caring for herself, the mother assures that the fetus is well-cared-for too.

TIM: Did you cut your hair? It looks good.

MITZI: I had it cut, styled, and henna'd. You like it?

TIM: Yeah.

MITZI:   It was weird.   I was at Southcenter returning something, and like boom, I walk into the Gene Juarez Salon and order everything!   I didn't even have any money!   Can you tell I had a makeover?

TIM:   Absolutely.

MITZI:   Turns out my skin tone isn't peach-based, it's actually part of the pink spectrum!

NITA:   Whatta shocker.

TIM:   How's the apartment?

MITZI:   Totally nice.   I'm painting everything yellow, you know?   Really, really like this warm, cervical yellow.   You gotta come down and see it.

*(Pause.  Tim nudges Nita.  She bats him off.)*

NITA:   You know, everybody's getting their forms together for the Esperanto World Congress in Poland this summer.

MITZI:   We can still go together.

NITA:   Will Chuck let you?

MITZI:   I'll only be like eight months or something, Nita. I'm not giving up my life.

*(Tim nudges Nita again.  She looks at him and then digs into her bag, pulls out a wrapped package, and puts it on the counter.)*

NITA: Here. It works. I tried it out last night.

MITZI: What is it?

NITA: Open it.

TIM: Oh honey, you don't know the torture we went through to get this! I actually walked into that breeder den-of-iniquity, Babies-R-Us.

NITA: He did. I got a picture. He was amazingly brave.

TIM: Oh my Loooorrd, what were they thinking? I've never seen primary colors abused to such a disastrous extent!

*(Mitzi opens the package. It is an electric breast pump.)*

MITZI: Whoa...! *(beat)* What is it?

NITA: Don't you know anything? It's an electric breast pump! You don't have to lift a finger.

TIM: Just a boob.

NITA: My sister has two, one for each tit. Saves time. Awesome, huh? Absolutely top-of-the-line.

TIM: *(turning it on)* Listen to this puppy!

*(There is a loud motor sound.)*

NITA: You didn't get one yet, did you?

MITZI: No.

NITA: Good, 'cause the motor on this thing, it's like BMW quality. And you're gonna LOVE the way it vibrates. *(she puts it up to her crotch)* Oh yeah...

TIM: Darling, please, you're at Subway.

MITZI: Wow. Thanks, you guys. This is like my first shower gift.

NITA: Yeah? *(this is an endearment)* Well, fuck you, sweetie.

MITZI: *(smiles)* Fuck you too.

*(Tim and Nita disappear. Mitzi takes off her Subway hat. Chuck approaches with a duffel bag over one shoulder. He hands her the pregnancy stick.)*

CHUCK: Here.

MITZI: What is it?

CHUCK: It's the stick we used, you know, to find out.

MITZI: What am I 'sposed to do with it?

CHUCK: You're the wife. You keep the mementos. He'll want this later. We gotta start a box. My mom's got one for me, back in St. Louis. Box full of my stuff, she saved everything. Even my first shit.

MITZI: Right.

CHUCK: She did. She said it didn't stink.

MITZI: *(teasing)* Oh, it didn't stink?

CHUCK: Well, according to her.

MITZI: *(sexy)* According to her, it still don't.

CHUCK: *(pulling her to him)* Noooo it don't... *(they kiss)* She said it smelled like vanilla. *(he rubs her lower tummy gently)* You mind if I feel him like this?

MITZI: Nope.

CHUCK: He's like a little rock in there.

MITZI: Yeah.

CHUCK: Harder than I thought he would be. You know, you see pregnant women, and their bellies look like they'd be soft, like pillows. But this is...

MITZI: Solid.

CHUCK: Yeah.

MITZI: Stubborn, like me.

CHUCK: Exactly. You sure this is how it's supposed to feel at 4 months?

MITZI: Nobody's raising any flags.

CHUCK: Huh.

MITZI: And I don't even puke up anymore.

CHUCK: You know, when I feel this, I think about being 8 years old and riding my dirt bike 'round and 'round this circuit we'd built in a vacant lot off Skinker Boulevard. We'd 360 off this plywood ramp, come down, surf the mud puddle, then up and over the hood of an old La Sabre, back down, around, do it again. Over and over, all day long. Just stop every so often to drink water out of this guy's hose. *(beat)* Sometimes I think those were the best days of my life... *(beat)* I got my orders. We move in 36 hours.

MITZI: What...?

CHUCK: They said they'd give us more notice, but they moved us up or something.

MITZI: 36 hours...?

CHUCK: Yeah, but they got this service now. We can talk to each other on TV or something. When you pick up the phone, you actually see who you're talking to. So I'll be able to watch you get all fat and happy.

MITZI: Great.

CHUCK: So, you know, it won't be so bad...

MITZI: No...

CHUCK: And you got your Copier Repair class and your Esperanto, right?

MITZI: Yeah.

CHUCK: And Subway and your Great Books and stuff.

MITZI: Sure.

CHUCK: Damn! I hate missing all this! I wanna know right away, right? I wanna see him first thing. Even if it's not your day, push your way to the front of the line. Tell the C.O., he'll understand, just get my kid in front of that camera for me, okay?

MITZI: You think you'll be gone that long?

*(Chuck shrugs. They hug, a bit awkward, and release. Chuck sniffs the air in the direction of Reckless Mary's stake.)*

CHUCK: I smell bacon again.

MITZI: Yeah. Me too…

*(They ponder this a moment. Then Chuck walks off with his duffel bag. Mitzi puts on her Subway hat, takes a pair of tongs and messes absentmindedly with her tomato slices, as Thomas Aquinas thunders ponderously up to the counter.)*

AQUINAS: Girl! Bring me a 12-inch Club before I faint!

MITZI: Mr. Aquinas…?

AQUINAS: And chips, by God!

MITZI: I thought you were on the Jared Diet Plan. You're supposed to order the 6-inch sandwich.

AQUINAS: *(waving this off)* 6-inch? That's like eating a flea.

MITZI: *(matter-of-fact)* Actually a 6-inch Club provides... *(she reads from a flyer)* '24 grams of protein, 46 grams of carbohydrates, and 6 grams of fat.

*(She tries to hand the leaflet to Aquinas, he bats it away.)*

AQUINAS: Blasphemy! I'm hungry! Super-size it.

*(Mitzi makes him a sandwich. He watches her work.)*

AQUINAS: My God, you people are infatuated with statistics. Do you know, where I come from, when we went to cook an animal, we cooked the WHOLE animal. We didn't dilly-dally with calorie counts. Take roast mutton. We'd go out to the fields, find a ram, kill it, skin it, slice it down the middle, clean it out, stuff it with breadcrumbs, oil, eggs, pepper, ginger, pounded almonds, braised chickens, pigeons, doves, other small fowl, rodents, whatever hadn't gone bad. Whatever would add to the succulence of the thing, you see. Then we'd sew the bloody thing back up and roast it until it was done! And when it was done, we pulled it out and WE ATE IT. No second thoughts. No regret, whatsoever! So, I urinate on Jared. I urinate on his diet. I would've fainted at prayers this morning if I'd continued to follow his anemic advice.

MITZI: Extra dressing?

AQUINAS: You bet. *(beat)* You've stopped coming to my Beginning Catholicism Forum. And you're pregnant.

MITZI: *(beat)* How do you know that?

AQUINAS: Twitch on my left side.

MITZI: Oh. Wow… Well, now that I'm having a baby, everybody says I've got to start, you know, making targeted life choices.

AQUINAS: Who says that?

MITZI: Nita. Chuck. My mom…

AQUINAS: And Esperanto seems more 'targeted' than Catholicism?

MITZI: It's not that I'm not interested in Catholicism, Mr. Aquinas. I am. I guess I just figured for right now — given what's going on in the world and how everybody's shouting at one another, and misunderstanding their points and everything — I thought a universal second language might be more practical.

AQUINAS: Ah. *(beat)* I suppose it's just as well… I almost quit last week.

MITZI: Catholicism?

AQUINAS: No-no, the forum. Walked right out the door. Left the little neophytes clutching their brand new plastic rosaries. *(shaking his head)* Converts. These days all we attract are the nitpickers. The ones that fixate on the details, like those calorie counts. But Catholicism is a metaphorical ANIMAL, you know? It's about big, messy ideas, like… Faith! And Love! And Eternal Damnation! Toss me a bag of Tim's Sea Salt and Vinegar. *(she throws him a bag of chips)*

MITZI: So what happened?

AQUINAS: It's not what *happened*, it's what's *happening*. Everything is so two-dimensional I can't stand it. For example, you should hear all the sanctimonious yakkity-yak about 'immediate hominization'.

MITZI: What's that?

AQUINAS: It's this inane position the church has taken lately that gives an embryo moral standing as a 'human person' from the moment of conception. It's ludicrous, but these new puppies are eating it up like kibble. Do you know, they actually began to argue with me – ME – when I tried to explain this was a recent, and in my opinion, theologically flawed change for the Church. They practically threw me out of my own classroom!

MITZI: Wow.

AQUINAS: I tell you, it's been quite difficult, hovering in the ether-world, watching some of our most enlightened principles get swept away.

MITZI: I think you'd be really good at Esperanto.

AQUINAS: I am Saint Thomas Aquinas! One of the most influential Catholics of the 2$^{nd}$ Millennium.

*(Reckless Mary charges across the stage with a Subway bakery tray.)*

MARY: Fresh-baked wheat rolls, comin' through!

AQUINAS:  My writings form the basis for much of what is considered standard Catholic theology.

MARY:  Fie!  There he be... bonin' on again.  *(shouting at Aquinas)*  I don't give a hoot about the Manichees, ya dumb ox!

AQUINAS:  So why is it that one of my most profound insights has about as much appeal with the Vatican today as a case of small pox?

MITZI:  What insight is that?

MARY:  The fact that he shits out his arse.

AQUINAS:  Delayed ensoulment.

MITZI:  Delayed ensoulment?

AQUINAS:  Yes.

MITZI:  That's not in the pamphlets.

AQUINAS:  My point exactly.  You've never heard of it because it's been buried like a corpse.  Shuttled quietly out of the room like the clergy's illegitimate offspring.  Can I have a Coke, please?

MITZI:  Pepsi okay?

AQUINAS:  *(shrugs his agreement, not thrilled with this option)*  Delayed ensoulment concerns the timing of when a potentially human conceptus becomes a human being, by receiving – from God – a soul.

MITZI: That happens, like, ASAP, right?

AQUINAS: No, no! You see? NOT at conception. God can only bestow such a gift on a being that has the faculties in place to receive it. I spell all of this out quite clearly in my seminal book: *Summa Contra Gentiles.* In which I agree with Aristotle and St. Augustine, that the human embryo must go through a series of stages; beginning with a vegetative state, leading to an animal state, and finally reaching a point at which it is physiologically ready and able to receive a human soul. Thus DELAYED -- not immediate -- ensoulment. This was confirmed as doctrine by the Catholic Church at the Council of Vienne, in 1312, and has been the dominant tradition in Christianity up until this blasted century. It is why we refused to baptize miscarriages and stillbirths. Because in the eyes of the church, they had not yet been endowed with the moral status of a human person.

*(Mitzi is quiet a moment, she finishes making his sandwich.)*

MITZI: I'm keeping my baby, Mr. Aquinas.

AQUINAS: I'm not suggesting you do anything else.

MITZI: *(putting his sandwich down)* 12-inch Club, extra dressing.

AQUINAS: Thank you, my dear. It's a masterpiece.

*(Aquinas eats his sandwich with relish. Mary returns to the safety of her stake and eyes him warily.)*

MARY: Look at 'im. You know why he's such a glutton? He's sexually frustrated. God's truth. Joined the fekkin' Dominican Order at seventeen, to burn us heretics and witches. But his mother, the Countess Theodora, couldn't stand his obnoxious piety, had 'im kidnapped and brought back home, where he was imprisoned in the family tower for over a year. *(dropping a little ancient gossip)* Some say his brothers sent a naked prostitute in, to tempt 'im with sins of the flesh. Poor dumb ox was so traumatized, he drove the drab out with a hot poker. After that, God took pity on 'im, sent two angels down with a chastity belt that would henceforth stop his lower regions from their divel yearnings, only to leave his mouth as open as you please...

MITZI: So when does it change?

AQUINAS: What?

MITZI: When is the fetus ready to receive a soul?

AQUINAS: Well, it depends.

MARY: Aye, "it depends." Takes 40 days fer males, but we females — bein' as how we spring from deformed male embryos — we stew a good *90 days*, before God grants us the dregs of a soul.

AQUINAS: But approximately, at quickening.

MARY: Quickenin', aye.

MITZI: Quickening.

*(Mitzi takes a sudden, surprised breath in, and looks down at her belly. The Expert and his podium light up.)*

EXPERT: So. Let's quickly recap fetal development. *(he may use some visual aid here)* Day 1. Sperm meets egg. 32 hours later the resulting zygote begins to divide and travel down the fallopian tube, where it will attach itself to the uterine wall around Day 8. At 6 weeks LMP, a rudimentary heart, head, and tail have formed, and the embryo is indistinguishable from the embryos of other mammals, including mice, pigs, and elephants. By 14 weeks arms, legs, feet, and hands are fully formed, and the fetus begins reflexive movements. At approximately 18 weeks, we have quickening.

MARY: Aye, quickenin'.

EXPERT: The point at which the mother can feel the movements of the fetus. Weeks 20 through 22, see the first synapses developing among neurons in the cortex, the area of the brain that deals with perception and thought. Questions?

AQUINAS: Is anything wrong?

MITZI: Oh. No. No, everything's actually... okay. *(beat)* Chuck's been gone two months already. I finished painting the apartment, it's all yellow now... the doors, the ceilings, the baby's room... everything... *(beat)* I've been thinking about moving back to my folk's place. At least 'til Chuck gets back.

AQUINAS: No disgrace in that.

MITZI: No, I guess not.

AQUINAS: There's something more…?

MITZI: *(there is)* No. Not really…

*(Aquinas waits. Mitzi wipes down the counters. The Expert starts up again.)*

EXPERT: In the weeks after quickening, we see a dramatic psychological shift in the gravida. As the fetus now begins to assert its individuality, with movements the mother can neither stop nor start, a gradual acceptance of, and love for, this new independent being begins. The female now endows the fetus with its own unique 'personality'.

MITZI: Mr. Aquinas, can I ask you something?

AQUINAS: Certainly.

EXPERT: Fantasies about who the baby is, its sex, and a wish for it to be perfect, are quite common. At the same time, fear of producing a defective child is universal. This fear is most often expressed through dreams of dead, deformed children, or scenes of mass destruction.

MITZI: What are you doing here?

AQUINAS: Why do you ask?

MITZI: Because… I'm just kind of wondering about my sanity. I'm having a lot of weird dreams. Like, I keep seeing this girl, right? In my dream. This girl with slurred speech and one side of her face droops, you know?     (continued)

MITZI (Cont'd): Like maybe someone poured battery acid on her or something. And she's so angry at me, like I did something to hurt her, or... I don't know. *(beat)* And I'm seeing an awful lot of you.

AQUINAS: That's not so scary, is it?

MITZI: It's not exactly normal.

AQUINAS: Yes, well, I understand your anxiety. But I've spent my life deliberating this question of existence, and the one thing I can tell you, Mitzi, is there's more play in the system than would appear.

MITZI: More play...?

AQUINAS: I'm talking about actual, flesh-and-blood, matter — by matter I mean you, those salami slices, that hat you're wearing. It's all really only a very small part of the entire existence equation.

MITZI: *(not seeing what this means)* Okay...

AQUINAS: So, it seems to me, given that the world is on such a shaky foundation, that I can be as real as you need me to be.

*(The way Aquinas says this makes Mitzi nervous.)*

MITZI: I don't understand. What does that mean?

*(Mitzi's cell phone starts to ring. MITZI waits for more of a response from AQUINAS but he picks crumbs from his plate, so she goes to answer the call, and when her back is turned, AQUINAS disappears.)*

MITZI: *(answering her cell phone)* Hello…?

DR. BLOCK: *(VO, on the phone)* Mitzi Mendoza?

MITZI: Yes?

DR. BLOCK: Mitzi, this is Dr. Block.

MITZI: *(not sure who this is)* Dr. Block?

DR. BLOCK: Yes. Your OB. You're pregnant, correct?

MITZI: Oh yeah, Dr. Block. Wow. Haven't seen you in awhile.

DR. BLOCK: Sorry about that. It's been quite hectic.

MITZI: That's okay. Thanks for checking in. Thing's are really humming along, she's kicking up a storm in there! And now that I'm pretty sure she's a girl, I've decided to re-paint her room a kind of dusky, intellectual purple. I'm not sure what Chuck's going think, but I don't know… the color just speaks to me, you know?

DR. BLOCK: Yes, well --

MITZI: And that nurse of yours, Song? Very on-the-ball. She's totally hip to everything that's happening, like all the stuff about my nipples being inverted? She's got me on this whole nipple-training program --

DR. BLOCK: *(breaking in)* Which is why I'm calling Mitzi. Song tagged your last measurements, and we're a little concerned.

MITZI: *(beat)* Concerned? Why?

DR. BLOCK: Well, at 6 months, we should really be seeing higher numbers, sternum to pelvic bone.

MITZI: Higher numbers...?

DR. BLOCK: More growth.

MITZI: Uh-huh.

DR. BLOCK: The baby should be bigger.

MITZI: I'm not as big-as-a-house, but Song said that's normal for a first pregnancy.

DR. BLOCK: I've gone ahead and scheduled you for an ultrasound.

MITZI: I thought you said I was young enough, I wouldn't need one?

DR. BLOCK: That was before. We just need to see what's going on in there.

MITZI: Yeah, but --

DR. BLOCK: Don't worry, ultrasounds are a piece of cake.

MITZI: But I'm not sure that TriCare covers that kind of thing, Dr. Block. They're not very big on the extras. And me and Chuck, we're on a pretty fixed income. I've already spent a lot more than I should've on paint.

DR. BLOCK: I'm sure it's covered if I order it, and I've ordered it. Roxbury Ultrasound. They're one floor down from my office. 10 am, tomorrow.

MITZI: Tomorrow? Isn't that kind of soon?

DR. BLOCK: I don't want you to worry about this, Mitzi. 'Failure to Grow' can be attributed to any number of things, not all of them significant.

MITZI: She's failing to grow?

DR. BLOCK: Go home, rent a movie, get your mind off it. Come in tomorrow and we'll see what's up. Okay?

MITZI: *(beat)* Sure. Okay.

*(Mitzi hangs up the phone. Reckless Mary pops her head up from behind her stake. Mitzi still doesn't hear her.)*

MARY: Sure... they got you now. They know how to sow the seeds of fear... He's made you a pawn on his chessboard, and now they get to start pokin'... Once they start that, sister, it's all over. Like pickin' a scab, they just pick, pick, pick.

*(Sergei, an ultrasound technician, sails toward Mitzi wheeling an ultrasound machine and an examining table. He wears a big, enthusiastic smile. Except for his medical terminology, his English is limited.)*

SERGEI: Ah! You are Mitzi?

MITZI: Yes.

SERGEI: Good! I am Sergei, yes? You will lie down please... *(indicating the examining table)* Shirt up! *(she does this, exposing her belly, he looks at her chart)* So! You are 22, yes?

MITZI: Yes.

SERGEI: Good! Very good time for babies, yes? Best time for babies, before 30! More energy, yes? More milk! My wife. 3 babies before 30. Good thing. Lots of energy! Lots of milk! *(pouring a clear gel onto her stomach and spreading it around)* This will feel cold!

MITZI: Ah!

SERGEI: *(eyeing her belly)* You are... four months, yes?

MITZI: Almost six.

SERGEI: *(surprised)* Six! Ah. Yes... *(he gets quieter, but keeps smiling)* Okay... Now I must look. No talk.

*(Sergei starts to move the probe around Mitzi's stomach. He watches his monitor intently, becoming anxious by what he sees, but he still continues to smile. Mary talks directly to Sergei, who does hear her.)*

MARY: Look at ya, grinnin' like an imp at the divel's tit...

SERGEI: *(still grinning at Mitzi, but talking to Mary)* What to do? You tell me? I am probing this Mitzi...

MARY: Incubus! Satan's barfly.

SERGEI: Low growth, it says, yes? No problem. Many times, this is nothing. But sometimes, it is not nothing. Sometimes, it is something. In this case... it is something. *(he rattles off a list of the anomalies he sees)* Cranial vault absent. Rudimentary brain tissue covered by membrane, not bone. Head flattened. Face has frog-like appearance, prominent bulging eyeballs. Associated polyhydrramios. High fetal activity.

MITZI: Whoa... are you catching that? She's kicking up a storm right now.

SERGEI: *(to Mitzi, big smile)* Yes! *(back to Mary)* And what to do? For me, Sergei? Keep smiling? I came in smiling. I am happy person. But now I see. Her baby severely deformed, yes? But how can I stop smiling? If I stop... she will know. Something very wrong! So I smile, yes?

MARY: Like a child of Bedlam.

SERGEI: This smiling, I hate. I hate this smiling.

*(Mitzi focuses on the technician as he works.)*

MITZI: Can you tell if it's a boy or girl...?

SERGEI: *(big grin)* No!

MARY: Ruddy liar.

MITZI: Really? I thought you guys could. *(he doesn't respond, just smiles, keeps working)*

MITZI: Well... she's okay, right? Just small or something. Maybe she'll be a gymnast. Dr. Block said --

SERGEI: I cannot diagnose, yes? *(he taps his name badge)* Technician! Not doctor!

MITZI: But, you must be seeing something...

SERGEI: No problem! Your doctor, explain everything!

MITZI: *(leaning forward)* Can I take a look...?

SERGEI: *(taking rapid, precise picture/clicks)* Just! Few! More! Points!

*(Mitzi watches Sergei more intently, she seems to know.)*

MITZI: *(quietly)* What are their names?

SERGEI: What?

MITZI: Your children. You said you have three.

SERGEI: I'm sorry. No...

MITZI: I'll bet they have great names.

SERGEI: Posterior fossa. *(click)* Cerebellum. *(click, click)*

MITZI: Something's wrong.

SERGEI: Spine.

MITZI: *(worried)* Something's wrong with my baby?

SERGEI:  Done!

*(Sergei wipes down the probe and places it beside the machine.)*

SERGEI: *(finally removing the smile, touching her arm)*  I phone.  Dr. Block.

*(The technician disappears, as Mitzi wipes the goop from her belly and slowly buttons her shirt.  Mary comes over and examines the ultrasound probe.)*

MARY:  This be the new model, I fathom.  Old one was longer, forged with Spanish iron.  The one that cam to my village with the White Coat already had a babe's blood on it.  He startin' pokin' it up womyn who were havin' hard birth.  "Be out of my way, hag!  I bear the forceps," he cried.  Army 'a White Coats sproutin' tools like chicken claws, smothered the land, killed off the midwife's magic.  Took from us our work, ourselves.  Those that turned a breech, they cut off their hands.  Those that spake the recipes, they ripped out their tongues.  Those that refused to cower in their skirts, that kept alive in their souls the wisdom of herbs and breath, those... they burned.

*(Mary goes back to her stake.  Mitzi has finished getting dressed, but she doesn't get up to go out.  She seems frozen, staring off.  Lights down on her and up on Vera, with a magazine, in the waiting room.  Nita comes in.)*

NITA:  Vera...?

VERA:  Well, hello there!

NITA: How's it going?

VERA: *(happy to have someone to talk to)* Oh, who the hell knows! I've been sittin' here in this waiting room for hours, reading about the next damn tragedy for Nicole Kidman. Mitz came outa that door white as a sheet. And suddenly everybody's got somethin' real important to do. They can't seem to spare the time to even look at us. Finally the receptionist hears from the good doctor. He tells us some definite concerns have arisen. He says get some lunch and meet him upstairs in their conference room in an hour. Get some lunch...

NITA: Where's Mitzi now?

VERA: *(pointing down a hall)* Peeing again. I remember this kinda limbo. I felt it years ago the night Putz-meier almost killed me with my own fuckin' iron. I was quick-like-a-bunny runnin' up the steps to the deck with him right on my tail, when he slips, and falls back down to the cement, flat on his back. I remember lookin' down at him, holding my breath... waitin' to see if he was gonna rise again.

*(A conference table shows up center stage. Mitzi, Vera, and Nita move to sit around it. Dr. Block enters, followed by Sheila Luffington, an overworked insurance adminis-trator. She's loaded down with files.)*

DR. BLOCK: Ah. Mitzi. There you are...

SHEILA: *(to Mitzi, shaking her hand)* Hi. Sheila Luff-ington, with TriCare. *(turning to Vera, doing the same)* Sheila Luffington, with TriCare.

VERA: Uh-huh.

SHEILA: *(shaking Nita's hand)* Sheila Luffington --

NITA: TriCare. Gotcha.

DR. BLOCK: Well, let's get started. Mitzi, we have some very bad news, so I'm not going to beat around the bush. The fetus you're carrying is textbook anencephalic. This was alarmingly clear to the Ultrasound Tech and caused quite a stir in their research department.

NITA: Anencephalic?

DR. BLOCK: Anencephaly being the congenital absence of the skull, the scalp and the forebrain or cerebral cortex. The brain stem is present and operating efficiently, controlling the autonomic nervous system. The basic functions. Heart beat, breathing, that sort of thing. Technically, the fetus is alive, but... with this level of deformity... without the cortex, it can't see, hear, or feel anything. And never will. In short, Mitzi, the diagnosis is fatal.

MITZI: *(barely audible)* Oh.

VERA: *(trying to catch up)* Are you saying her kid doesn't have a brain?

DR. BLOCK: Basically, yes.

MITZI: Well... that can't be right. I mean, maybe that guy made a mistake or something? He wasn't from here.

NITA: What about one of those shunts? My neighbor's kid had water-on-the-brain, they did one of those shunts.

DR. BLOCK: Unfortunately, in this case, there's nothing to shunt. If this fetus does survive to term, it will die within days.

*(Dr. Block gives Mitzi a moment to absorb this.)*

MITZI: But... Dr. Block, this doesn't make any sense. I mean, she's so healthy, she's kicking me all the time.

DR. BLOCK: That's quite characteristic. The remnants of it's brain are exposed and... well, there's often a high level of reflexive muscle movements.

NITA: Oh my God.

DR. BLOCK: *(clearing his throat, forging ahead)* Our best course, at this point, is to induce labor now, before we wind up with further complications.

*(Sheila finally speaks up.)*

SHEILA: Ah, Dr. Block.

DR. BLOCK: Yes?

SHEILA: Hi. Um, I'm Sheila Luffington with TriCare? We don't work with you much, so you may be unaware of our current policies.

DR. BLOCK: What policies?

SHEILA: Well, I know this may sound a bit... inopportune, but, if termination is your recommendation regarding this pregnancy, then we're going to have a problem on the insurance front.

DR. BLOCK: What do you mean? What kind of problem?

SHEILA: Well, you see Mitzi is only insured through her husband, John –

MITZI: Chuck. His name is Chuck.

SHEILA: Chuck. And therefore she's a military dependent covered by TriCare Management Activity.

DR. BLOCK: *(impatient)* Yes.

SHEILA: So... and I personally hate this, I really do. In fact, I spit on this policy. See? *(Sheila spits on her files)* Spit. Right there. But it's a rising tide, you know? What can one worn-out PCM do? When the folks up in HRA are putting out this kind of high-level restrictive MDR guidelines? We're all just SOOL.

NITA: Shit out of luck.

SHEILA: Exactly.

DR. BLOCK: I still don't see what you're getting at.

SHEILA: Here's the deal, Doctor. You're ordering Mitzi's labor be induced.

DR. BLOCK: Yes.

SHEILA: Well, technically, that's considered a late-term abortion.

MITZI: An abortion? I don't want an abortion.

DR. BLOCK: This is a medical decision, Mitzi. Remember that. *(to Sheila, a warning)* The semantics here are very important for the mental health of my patient, Sheila.

SHEILA: I understand, Dr. Block, but technically, this is an abortion, and according to the coverage rules set down by the 106$^{th}$ Congress, TriCare is prohibited from funding abortion services for any reason, including fatal prenatal anomalies, unless — or until -- that anomaly puts the woman's life in danger.

DR. BLOCK: Ms. Luffington, this diagnosis is incompatible with life. Not only that... but it's the maturing fetal cortex that instigates the onset of labor. Without a forebrain, and no ability to induce, Mitzi's pregnancy could last over a year.

SHEILA: I know that.

DR. BLOCK: So, you're asking her to knowingly continue to carry a dying fetus for 3 months *or longer*? This has got to be an exception!

SHEILA: No, unfortunately, it's not. There aren't *any* exceptions. Now, as far as I can tell... although grievous and abominably sad, Mitzi's pregnancy will not kill her. *(trying to be helpful)* I should mention that this 'denial of coverage' could be – and has been – successfully contested in court a few times, but only on a case-by-case basis. (continued)

SHEILA (Cont'd): This means Mitzi would need to find and pay for an attorney willing to fight for her right to abort.

DR. BLOCK: Induce.

SHEILA: Whatever. Mitzi, do you have an attorney?

MITZI: My head hurts.

SHEILA: And, as this condition is quite severe, there's also the chance the anomaly will wind up in demise before the legal entanglements have been fully resolved.

MITZI: Anomaly...

SHEILA: So, in short, I would suggest Mitzi, that you try and find a way to cover this procedure out-of-pocket. A realistic cost-estimate for an induced prostaglandin delivery -- assuming two days in the hospital and no serious complications -- is about $10,000.

NITA: Ten thousand dollars?!

SHEILA: Give or take.

VERA: So... whoa, whoa, whoa. Are you sayin' my daughter's gotta carry this thing around like a sack of rotting potatoes until she actually drops it?

SHEILA: If you'd asked me about the initial ultrasound, we would have denied it, and then you wouldn't have known there was anything wrong with it until birth.

MITZI: It...

NITA: And that's better?

MITZI: It.

SHEILA: Maybe it is... given the circumstances.

DR. BLOCK: Look, Ms. Luffington, if this fetus does survive birth, the government is looking at an astronomic neonatal intensive care bill.

SHEILA: Yes, I'm aware of that. But postpartum is a much lower-profile playing field. If Mitzi can't get the cash together and winds up delivering, then we'd simply call for a 'DNR'.

NITA: 'DNR'?

DR. BLOCK: 'Do Not Resuscitate' order.

SHEILA: Takes longer, and is possibly more cruel to the neonate, but at least it's something we cover.

DR. BLOCK: This is insane.

SHEILA: I told you, Doctor, I spit on this policy.

DR. BLOCK: Is the Board at this hospital aware of these parameters? Because I think —

SHEILA: *(interrupts him with the sound of a game show buzzer)* BZZZZ! Been there. Done that. No change.

MITZI: *(low, to Sheila)* Don't call her an 'it'.

SHEILA: Pardon me?

MITZI: You called her an 'it'. Don't do that. She's a child. I want you to call her a child.

VERA: Oh for chrissake Mitzi, that's the last --

SHEILA: Anomaly, fetal demise, I'll call her whatever you want.

MITZI: *(insistent)* Child.

DR. BLOCK: *(beat, gently)* Son.

MITZI: *(beat)* What…?

DR. BLOCK: You're carrying a little boy.

*(The scene seems to blow up and disperse. Nita joins Tim, they sit. They're on a bus. Nita carries a boom box.)*

NITA: Oh-my-God, oh-my-Goooddd, Tim, it's so disgusting!

TIM: I know it's disgusting.

NITA: $10,000?! And they've got to try and raise that themselves? The military won't cover it?! Everybody else's insurance covers it. Blue Cross, Aetna, Group Health.

TIM: Oh honey, those guys would *love* to cover this, saves them a shitload of money in the end. Insurance companies make me gag.

NITA: And I mean... *(The bus stops. An older woman gets on with a shopping bag, and sits behind Tim and Nita)* This is what I mean, Tim. Here's this kid in the Army, defending our country from God-knows-what. He's making less than shit, he's putting his life on the line, and the U.S. Military can't see it's way clear to come forward and end his wife's suffering? It makes me sick!

TIM: I know it makes you sick.

NITA: I mean, Jesus, this is very rapidly becoming NOT my country!

TIM: Nita, don't start --

NITA: *(growing louder)* It's like all of a sudden we're DROWNING in conservative Republicans and their tiny, little dicks. They got Viagra covered by Medicare just like that. One quick stroke of their TINY, LITTLE DICKS. But birth control pills?! Therapeutic abortions?!

TIM: *(looking around, a warning)* This isn't the '2', dear, it's the bus to Burien.

NITA: *(rolling into a thick Texas accent)* Whoa now pardner, hold up dere... how is this gonna help my tiny little dick? Hmmm?! And if'n it ain't gonna help my tiny little dick, if'n it's gonna HINDER the effects of my tiny little dick, than -- hang on a minute -- we better make this little line-item outa pocket! Can't fund everything now can we?

TIM: *(to the woman in a seat behind him)* She can go on like this for hours.

NITA: 'Cause'n we Republicans --

TIM: It's the main reason she's still single.

NITA: We like to see the RESULTS of what we fuck. That's right boy.

TIM: Nita.

NITA: We wanna UNLOAD our tiny little dicks on Iraq!

TIM: Nita, dear.

NITA: And the unemployed.

TIM: Time for juice and cookies.

NITA: And all those uppity women tryin' to sink their devil nails into this country. We say, 'you any kind of American lady, you gonna lay back, spread 'em, and shut the fuck up. Bella Abzug is DEAD, bitch! Get over it!'

TIM: *(clamping his hand over her mouth)* Would you just, please, STOP NOW?!

*(The woman behind has pulled the bell to stop the bus. She gets off. Tim cautiously pulls his hand away Nita's mouth.)*

NITA: *(stunned)* You put your hand over my mouth.

TIM: Yes.

NITA: Why'd you do that?

TIM: Nita…

NITA: What?

TIM: I'm just… sick of how easy all this is for you.

NITA: All what?

TIM: This! *(lowering his voice)* What we're talking about. Getting rid of babies.

NITA: Are you saying…? *(beat)* Oh-my-God, you're one of THEM?

TIM: Nita.

NITA: You're John Ashcroft?!

TIM: No.

NITA: Anita Bryant!

TIM: Would you just listen --

NITA: You don't think Mitzi should do this?!

TIM: No, I –

NITA: You don't?

TIM: No, I DO. It's just… I don't think you can --

NITA:  What?

TIM:  Nita, she's SIX MONTHS ALONG.

NITA:  So?

TIM:  So, that's a baby in there!  It's not some piece of glop!  Now, I know Mitzi's kid is totally messed-up.

NITA:  TOTALLY.

TIM:  But I don't think you can apply this same rule to every person who —

NITA:  Whoa, whoa.  You're climbing a verrrry slippery slope.

TIM:  Well, personally, I don't think it's so crazy to be cautious about this.

NITA:  Tim, you're scaring me.

TIM:  When I first came out to my father —

NITA:  Please, don't change the subject --

TIM:  *(insistent)*  When I came out, we were having an argument, and granted I kind of threw it at him, but one of the things that slipped out of his mouth was: "I wish you'd never been born."

NITA:  Bullshit, your dad's totally cool with it.

TIM: Yeah, he is. NOW. But he didn't really have a choice, did he? I was already AROUND. Look to the future, honey. One of these days they'll come up with some queer gene, right? And the minute they do, you KNOW they're gonna start testing people for it.

NITA: I can't believe I'm hearing this.

TIM: What if some red-state Bob-and-Nancy find out the kid they're carrying has a 92% chance of being gay? Do you really think for one minute they'd keep it, given an option?

*(Nita is stumped)*

NITA: Tim.

TIM: They don't keep their Down Syndrome kids.

NITA: Yeah, but –

TIM: Hell, dear, in China and India they've gotten rid of so many girl-babies, the countries are crawling with bachelors.

NITA: Well, people don't do that here.

TIM: Really? How do you know?

NITA: You are so Oliver-Stoning this entire —

TIM: And for that matter, we haven't even TOUCHED on the profit-motive yet. What if somebody's having a kid with some congenital-whatever that's gonna cost their *insurance company* an exorbitant amount once it's born?

NITA: Oh my God, we're back to insurance!

TIM: You think that health provider is not going to try and exert at least a LITTLE pressure on that mother to abort? You think they're going to throw their arms around her and say: "Please, keep the kid! Cost us millions!"

NITA: I am NOT listening to this.

*(Nita turns away from Tim, putting her fingers in her ears and humming loudly.)*

TIM: *(over her humming)* It ain't gonna happen, honey, believe me! I've seen how they handle people with expensive diseases.

NITA: *(out the window)* Oh shit. Fucking great.

*(Nita grabs the boombox and stands up.)*

TIM: What?

NITA: That was 128th. We missed our stop!

*(Lights out as Nita and Tim scramble off the bus, up on The Expert at his podium.)*

THE EXPERT: At this juncture, we –

*(The Expert's cell phone rings once, but stops. The Expert begins again.)*

THE EXPERT: It is at this particular juncture –

*(The cell phone rings again. The Expert answers quickly.)*

THE EXPERT: *(into cell phone)* Yes? *(listens)* Was my wife not clear on this point? *(listens)* I see your situation but that is not our problem. Now, I'm in the middle of a lecture – No, they are not 'big shreds', they are CLUMPS *(listens)* No, and not only that, I expect to find shredded bark on my lawn by this evening, or we go to court.

*(The Expert hangs up the phone and continues.)*

THE EXPERT: THUS, Mitzi's standard psychic gestation has jumped the tracks. Confronted by her offspring's imminent fetal demise, the gravida finds herself in a precarious psychological predicament and responds, using the following 6-stage process. Quickly summarized, this includes: numbness, anger, anticipatory grief, psychological withdrawal from the still-living fetus, feelings of guilt and failure, and an overwhelming urge to flee the situation, as if physical relocation will somehow distance her from the given circumstances.

*(Lights out on the The Expert. Mitzi and Vera stand side-by-side. Vera starts to cross the stage, Mitzi doesn't move.)*

VERA: Mitzi, this is the Safeway. We need to pick up onions, chicken thighs, and Rudolfo's special dental floss. You wanna come in with me to the Safeway?

MITZI: You go ahead. I'll just stand here by the car.

VERA: The car don't need your help.

MITZI: *(beat)* Can we go for a drive?

VERA: We're on a drive.

MITZI: I mean, like a trip.

VERA: *(beat)* Where do you wanna go?

MITZI: Mt. St. Helens.

VERA: Mt. St. Helens? What for?

MITZI: I wanna see devastation. Real devastation. I wanna see something that's had its head blown all the way off.

VERA: *(not sure how to respond)* Uh-huh… well… you go ahead and stand there then.

*(Vera walks off. Mitzi is handed a bathrobe, she puts it on. A door bell rings. Nita and Tim burst in, with a boom box.)*

TIM: Hey there, girlie! It's your Gay-and-Bisexual-Esperanto–Support-Group!

NITA: On a house call!

TIM: Step back, honey. 'Cause we're about to put a little sparkle in your day! Hit the button, Nita.

*(Nita hits the button. We hear a karaoke background tape of 'Those Were the Days, My Friend'. Tim and Nita sing the melody in Esperanto, complete with dance steps. They've worked on this.)*

TIM: ESTAS BON-TAVERNO EN LA URBO

NITA: KIE KUTIME SIDAS CIUJ NI

TIM: POR DISKUTI REVOJN DE FUTURO

NITA: KAJ TRINKI EL KALIKOJ DU AU TRI

TIM & NITA:  LA GAJAJ TAGOJ LA
       PASINTAJ TEMPOJ JA
       KIAM NI KANTIS DANCI POR KAPRIC
       NI VOLIS KAPTI CION
       DE MONDTREZORO KIO
       EKZISTIS NUR POR NIA FORFELIC!
       LA LA LA LA LA LA, LA LA LA LA LA LA,
       LA GAJAJ TAGOJ DE LA BONA VIV!

*(They end with a flourish and disappear, as Mitzi turns and calls out for Aquinas.)*

MITZI: *(urgent)* Mr. Aquinas...? Mr. Aquinas, are you here?

*(She waits, looks around for him. Reckless Mary pokes her head up from behind her stake and for the first time Mitzi can see her.)*

MARY: He be unclothed, at the gymnasium. Workin' on his fekkin abs.

MITZI: Who... who are you?

MARY: Reckless Mary. Scottish midwife. Died 1662, may I rest in peace.

MITZI: Oh. *(touching her nose)* You smell awful.

MARY: Part of me penance. Standard package. *(indicating her belly)* He still kickin'?

MITZI: Yes. *(beat)* I was looking for Mr. Aquinas...

MARY: Aye, so ye said. What might such a lass be wantin' with that windbag?

MITZI: I want to confess something.

MARY: Ah.

MITZI: Do you take confessions?

MARY: *(thinks about this)* In a manner 'a speakin'. A laborin' womyn'll moan all sorts of dark things after awhile.

MITZI: Will you hear mine?

MARY: Mmmmm... alright... but don't be all day.

MITZI: Okay. *(she takes a breath, then starts)* See... when it really sunk in... you know, about what Dr. Block was telling me... about how messed up my baby was...?

MARY: Aye...

MITZI: *(this is a hard thing to say)* I wanted him out. Like, right away. I didn't want to patch him up. Every part of me was practically screaming to get him gone. And... I felt almost lucky. (continued)

MITZI (Cont'd): About his missing an entire brain or whatever, because that kind of problem seems pretty hopeless, you know? I mean, what if it had been something less clear-cut? Like, no arms or something? *(beat)* I don't think I'd want to keep him then, either.

MARY: *(with kindness)* So it would seem...

MITZI: I didn't know this about myself. That this urge to get rid of him would be so huge. I mean, I consider myself a good person, you know? And whenever I imagined something like this in my head, I always handled it so well! I was, like, sad, and yet serene and resigned, you know? And I was gonna do whatever it took, for my baby...

MARY: Aye...

MITZI: I mean, until they point it out to you on the screen, all the bulging eyes and bits of mangled... I don't think you can really know what you'd do... or even who you are...

MARY: That's right, sister. That be God's truth. Nuthin' to be ashamed of. Yer body be reactin' that way, naturally. Sure as daylight. 'Ats ets job, takin' care of you. It's bellowin': "Save the resources! Shut it down! Shore it up for the next attempt!"

MITZI: Yeah...

MARY: But yer heart...

MITZI: Yes.

MARY: That squirrelly organ takes a different path. Et's a muscle that already knows this babe, loves 'im like a lamb. The heart be a river what won't reverse its flow. So it loves. And it loves until the womb be swept clean, and so, so far beyond. And there ye be, eh sister? Floatin'... burstin' with both sun and rain, like a blown-up sheep's bladder. Now yer knowin' those animal mothers that, in an act of pure kindness, devour their runts with no remorse. Now ye kin how they can do that...

*(A giant TV screen lights up. Chuck, in huge proportions, is pictured on it. He sees Mitzi.)*

CHUCK: *(calling)* Hey, Mitzi! Mitz!

*(Mary disappears.)*

CHUCK: Over here!

*(Mitzi walks over to the screen.)*

MITZI: Chuck...?

CHUCK: Hey.

MITZI: Hey.

*(Pause)*

MITZI: So... did the Captain tell you... about....?

CHUCK: Yeah.

MITZI: Yeah.

*(Pause)*

CHUCK:  Is he still kicking?

MITZI:  Yeah.

CHUCK:  Good. Fight to the finish. That's my boy.

MITZI:  Yeah... *(she cries)*

CHUCK:  Hey... Hey Mitzi, it's okay. I'm not mad. I mean it's not your fault, right?

MITZI:  My fault...?

CHUCK:  I mean you took all your vitamins and stuff.

MITZI:  Yeah...

CHUCK:  So, you know, hand of God. We'll just be a little more careful next time.

*(Pause)*

CHUCK:  I'm just saying we'll... you know... monitor things better.

*(Pause)*

MITZI:  How is it?  Over there...

CHUCK:  Okay. Sorta. So far, we've been spared check-point duties. But there's still no fucking refrigeration. All the Diet Cokes are lukewarm and shit... Tastes weird...

MITZI: Yeah.

CHUCK: My unit's pretty cool, though. We got a great C.O. Things are by-the-book, you know? Everybody knows what to expect.

MITZI: Yeah.

*(Pause)*

MITZI: Dr. Block wants me to terminate.

CHUCK: I heard that.

MITZI: But TriCare won't pay for it.

CHUCK: Yeah. Good for them.

MITZI: Why do you say that?

CHUCK: Why? Baby, it's abortion.

*(Pause)*

MITZI: I want to terminate, Chuck.

CHUCK: No. C'mon baby, just hang on, it's only a couple of months.

MITZI: But I need to.

CHUCK: No. No. I'm not aborting my kid. And I sure as hell ain't gonna pay for someone who does.

MITZI: But you don't know what this is like.

CHUCK: Sure I do.

MITZI: No, Chuck, I know why he's kicking. He could die anytime.

CHUCK: Fuck, we could *all* die anytime.

MITZI: And then he'd be floating around inside me, dead, this dead –

CHUCK: Look, don't think that way! I mean, yeah Mitz, you know? You got screwed. WE got screwed. And now you gotta do something you don't wanna do. So fucking what? Me too. You know? Look at me. I'm here doing stuff I don't wanna do.

MITZI: But Chuck –

CHUCK: No, please. Lemme just say this. See… this is our kid, and I need to think of him back there. I need to think that what I'm doing is feeding him, keeping him alive… and, and you too. I got an image of him, you know? A picture. And I gotta keep focused on that picture right now… or…

MITZI: Or what?

CHUCK: I dunno. I dunno, Mitz.

*(Pause)*

MITZI: The doctor –-

CHUCK: Doctors don't know shit.

MITZI; But maybe Chuck —

CHUCK: They don't know shit, Mitz.

MITZI: I'm just saying, maybe it's kinder to let him go.

CHUCK: That's bullshit, baby, don't kid yourself.

MITZI: But, I can't just --

CHUCK: Sure you can! I'm telling you to!

*(Pause)*

CHUCK: It's gonna be okay, baby. Just a minor set-back. Soon as I get back there, we'll make another one, okay?

*(Pause)*

CHUCK: Okay?

MITZI: *(quieter)* I gotta go.

CHUCK: Mitzi? Don't… don't do anything stupid, you hear me?

MITZI: Bye Chuck.

*(Mitzi walks away from the screen.)*

CHUCK: Mitzi…? Mitz!

*(Chuck disappears too. Lights up on Vera, feeling awkward and defiant, standing at a podium.)*

VERA:  Well, I just want to thank the Elders here at High-line Four Square Church for letting me come before you and say my peace.  First off... lemme just confirm... that I'm not a good Christian.  I do best, what I can.  But I've been lapsed ten years or so.  Don't know why, exactly.  Nothin' phenomenal happened.  Just stopped drivin' in this direction.  Seemed like a time management issue more'n anything else.  'Cause Mitzi was turnin' thirteen and it got too hard to drag her ass down here for Sunday school, and I'm not excusing myself, I'm just... explaining.    Because now I'm back, talking to you about my girl... *(hesitates, then just says it)*  She's twenty-two and she needs a late-term abortion, which her insurance won't cover and we can't pay for.  So.  *(angry)*  Any of you wanna snicker?  Wanna tell me it's just what I deserve, go right ahead, and I'll slap you straight to the hereafter.

*(Vera hadn't intended to get so confrontational, she mentally re-groups, tries to be more civil.)*

VERA:  'Cause, personally, I'm against abortion.  For most people.  But like it explains on the pink flyers, this isn't your run-of-the-mill... *(her patience wanes again)*  Look, I'll just be honest.  I came here to beg.  We need $10,000 and we don't got it.  And I'm going around my community, groveling like a bum, 'cause it's easier than watching my pregnant kid sit there catatonic in my living room.  I'd rather be anywhere but there.  Even here, among all you snot-nosed Christians.  So.  Here I am.  You got $10,000 or some fraction you'd care to give us, come on down after Pastor Mike completes this service.  That's it.  That's all I got.

*(Vera stomps off the podium. Dr. Block comes up to Mary's stake, he's got Mitzi's chart under one arm. He lights a cigarette and smokes. Mary appears.)*

MARY: No smokin', White Coat. Fire be no friend here.

DR. BLOCK: Oh, sorry.

*(Dr. Block puts out the cigarette. He takes her in.)*

DR. BLOCK: Those third-degree burns...?

MARY: The vast majority.

DR. BLOCK: What do you... use on them?

MARY: Me own remedy. Goat fat and gunpowder.

DR. BLOCK: Huh...

MARY: What ye got there? *(indicating the file)*

DR. BLOCK: Oh. Mitzi's chart...

MARY: Ah, I kin the girl.

DR. BLOCK: Yeah? Well... I wish I didn't. I hate cases like this. Don't get me wrong, it's just... I'm actually... *(he stops, looks at Mary)* Never mind.

MARY: *(coaxing him)* Nobody here but a divel's handmaid...

DR. BLOCK: *(making sure they're alone)* I'm thinking about bypassing her insurance restrictions.

MARY: Bypassin'? How?

DR. BLOCK: *(beat)* Fraud.

MARY: Fraud? *(excited)* Be that bad...?!

DR. BLOCK: If you're caught.

MARY: Could ye burn for that?

DR. BLOCK: I could lose my fucking license.

MARY: *(facetious)* Oh... ohhh... such a shame.

DR. BLOCK: Sure, go ahead and joke... *(pissed about this, getting it off his chest)* But explain to me why doctors are the only ones taking the fall here! Huh? I didn't invent these diagnostics. I'm not the guy billing them out at 200% of cost. But I am the one that's got to face the patient when the tests come back disastrous.

MARY: *(commiserating)* Poor White Coat. Now you're knowin' the bald, ugly truth about birth and death and the shadiness between 'em.

DR. BLOCK: I mean, it's my license on the line! I've got two kids that want to go to college! I've got a mortgage the size of Baltimore. Why are there *still* no humane parameters for handling the ethical firestorms these machines are so good at uncovering?!

MARY: *(with a certain sensuality)* In frightened times, people are suckled by the tiniest of absolutes. 'This be good, that be bad. This witch'll float, that one won't.' *(beat, eyeing his hospital coat)* Never wore a white coat myself...

DR. BLOCK: *(beat)* Would you... like to try it on?

MARY: Aye...

*(Dr. Block, debonair, removes his coat and helps Mary into it.)*

MARY: *(overwhelmed)* Ohhhh... Such fine cloth!

DR. BLOCK: Yes.

MARY: A linen, I think...?

DR. BLOCK: A cotton blend.

MARY: *(impressed)* A cotton blend...!

*(There is a definite attraction. Mary tries to keep it professional)*

MARY: What be your form of expulsion?

DR. BLOCK: Well... I'm thinking induction. Make sense?

MARY: Potions? Aye. Shame she's got to endure it.

DR. BLOCK: Yeah, I thought about that, but it's too late for a D & E.

MARY: Aye.

DR. BLOCK: Besides... I'm saying her water broke.

MARY: Ah, the fraud.

DR. BLOCK: Yes...

*(On an impulse, Dr. Block reaches out and touches the burns on her forearm. Mary lets him feel them a moment, then moves off, showing off the lab coat.)*

MARY: So... how am I to your eyes? Good?

DR. BLOCK: *(beat)* Aye. Good...

*(They disappear together. Lights up on Vera, as she knocks on Mitzi's door.)*

VERA: Mitz? *(the door opens)* Dr. Block called. He says he's figured out how to handle our insurance problems, turns out it's all in the coding. He's got a spot for you tomorrow morning.

MITZI: What?

VERA: I guess the sooner the better. Now, come on downstairs. You gotta be at the hospital by 6 am, and it's the same deal as when we spayed Princess, no food or water after midnight. So I thought you'd better have a good meal tonight.

MITZI: A last supper.

*(Vera can't take any more sadness.)*

VERA: Now just stop that, you hear me! I'm doin' all I can. I ordered Chinese. Your favorite. *(calming down)* And your friends are here... And your Uncle Tub showed up for the first time in two years, naturally. So, he's here too. Lord help us...

*(A table rolls in with everyone around it. Tim, Nita, and Uncle Tub. Vera and Mitzi join them. Vera empties a big plastic bag filled with Chinese take-out.)*

UNCLE TUB: *(mid-conversation)* -- and that's how I made all my money!

TIM: Artificial arms?

UNCLE TUB: You two are in luck, 'cause I happen to be wearing the arm that made me famous. This model is what we call our Mid-Finger Salute. *(to Vera)* You already tell 'em about this Vera?

VERA: Hadn't come up, Tub.

TUB: *(slightly hard of hearing)* What?

VERA: No.

TUB: You're gonna love this. Big with the Vietnam Vets. Notice the slightly enlarged middle finger. *(he holds up his left arm, it's artificial, with the fingers shaped in a permanent 'fuck you' position)*

VERA: *(lifting food cartons out of the bag)* Okay, mu shu chicken, with the funny pancakes.

TUB: We can do either arm, right or left. Same price.

VERA: Chinese... broccoli? Twice-cooked pork. Scallops in oysters sauce, steamed rice, and... something sweet-n-sour.

TUB: That's for me. Where's Rudolfo?

VERA: On a job.

TUB: What?

VERA: *(louder)* On a job!

TUB: He's still in the roofin' business?

VERA: Yep.

TUB: *(eyeing Nita, leans toward her, debonair)* Did Vera mention I'm single and active...?

VERA: Tub, these are Mitzi's friends. They came to support her. You be single and active somewheres else.

TUB: Support her? What's she need support for? *(looking at Mitzi and the others)* Why the pouts? You all look like you got worms. *(to Mitzi)* And you. Vera says you're pregnant. I thought women were 'sposed to blossom in pregnancy? When are you due, anyway?

MITZI: Tomorrow.

TUB: Tomorrow?! What're you gonna have? An orange? You got no big belly. Just like my first old lady. She had a kid on speed, holy shit, whatta fuckin' mess!

MITZI: *(not loud)* I'm being induced.

TUB: Wha -- a papoose? What she'd do, Vera? Fuck an Indian?

VERA: Tub, she said induced.

TUB: Excuse? No excuses necessary! I've fucked some fine Indian babes. Did I tell you, Vera? 'Bout that summer I was sellin' arms outside Spokane –

MITZI: *(interrupting him)* I said INDUCED.

VERA: Mitz…

TUB: 'Induced'? What does that mean?

MITZI: It's like an abortion.

TUB: What?

NITA: It is an ABORTION.

TUB: Abortion?!

VERA: *(loud enough so he gets her the first time)* There's something wrong with it! Now let's talk about something else!

TUB: What? What's wrong with it? It's probably just small. Hell, I was small once, nobody induced me! See, that's what's wrong with this country, Vera. Everybody's gotta have things perfect. Where's the rice? *(Tub scoops himself some rice)* Well, me and my buddies didn't go all the way to 'Nam just so a buncha goddamn, hoity-toity American women can be free to flush our genetic hopefuls right down the toilet! Bella Abzug bit the big one, babe. Get over it!

VERA: Tub, shut up!

*(Nita gets up, throws Tim a vindicated look.)*

NITA: *(to Vera)* Where's your bathroom? *(she exits in disgust)*

TUB: Pass the sweet and sour!

VERA: You don't know the whole story.

*(Tub starts spearing pieces of meat out of a take-out container with his middle finger.)*

TUB: And I don't wanna know! The 'whole story'. Whatta crock! That 'grey area' shit don't amount to a hilla beans in front of our lord-and-savior. Birth is birth, and death is death, and — what the fuck kinda meat is this, Vera? Pork?

VERA: That's tofu, Tub.

TUB: What?

VERA: TOFU.

TUB: See! *(waving this at them, as if this makes his point)* See! I rest my case!

VERA: GOOD.

TUB: *(beat)* But... you of all people, Vera. I mean, after all...

VERA: That's enough, Tub.

TUB: If it wudn't for me and Putzmeier draggin' your ass outa that clinic in Fresno —

VERA: That's a lie! I just went in there for some information.

TUB: Oh yeah. Information. Like how do I go about —

VERA: And that is PRIVATE! PRIVATE, TUB. Not yours to bring up! Now! We're all here for Mitzi! This is MITZI'S DINNER. Mitzi... go ahead, and say something...

*(All heads turn to Mitzi. She opens her mouth, shuts it again. Gets up and walks to the other side of the stage. The Nurse comes on, dragging an old, wooden labor chair. Vera trails behind Mitzi.)*

NURSE: And in through here...

VERA: Where are we? Are we still in the hospital?

NURSE: It's part of the old East Wing.

MITZI: So, I'm not in Maternity?

NURSE: Oh no, honey. We don't put cases like yours in Maternity, for everyone's sanity.

MITZI: Oh.

NITA: *(hands her a hospital gown)* Go ahead and take your clothes off, put this gown on, ties in back.

*(Mitzi goes off to change. Vera wanders the room)*

VERA: Feels awful cold. Is there heat?

NURSE: Of course. But you're right. Not a lot of bells and whistles in this department. It's old, but it's what we've got. We stick to the tried and true, when we're dealing with what we're dealing with here. Just get through it, honey. *(leaving)* Open the door when you're ready for me...

*(The Nurse exits. Mitzi comes back on.)*

MITZI: I thought I'd be in Maternity. They've got these great hot tubs and stuff...

VERA: Yeah. *(looking out the window)* Alley view...

MITZI: *(pointing to the labor chair)* What's that?

VERA: *(sees the chair)* Jesus, they musta pulled it outa some museum. It's a labor chair. They were ancient when I had you. Works like a potty chair for kids, only... you know...

MITZI: I'm not sitting on that to have my baby.

VERA: I'm sure they're not expecting you to. *(reconsidering)* Although. Dr. Block did say this takes some time. Having gravity on your side helps... you know... to keep things headed in the right direction. Maybe it'll come in handy.

MITZI: Not for me...

*(The Expert appears at his podium.)*

THE EXPERT: Anticipatory grief eventually turns into the real thing as the termination proceeds. Given the fact that Mitzi is well over 20 weeks, a less traumatic D & E must be ruled out, in favor of an Intraamniotic Instillation, otherwise known as a saline abortion. The procedure occurs as follows: the patient is given copious amounts of 'twilight' anesthesia, her cervix is softened and encouraged to open, using repeated insertions of sponge-like sticks called lamanaria. A needle is inserted into the uterine cavity and withdraws approximately 200 milliliters of amniotic fluid. A corresponding amount of 20% hypertonic saline solution is then injected back into the uterus. The fetal heartbeat generally stops within a few hours. The woman then goes into labor and delivers the dead fetus within 24 to 72 hours.

*(The Expert's cell phone rings, he turns it off.)*

THE EXPERT: Prostaglandin gels, and Pitocin, are often used to stimulate uterine contractions and help shorten the injection to delivery time.

*(Lights up on Mitzi, as she lays in a fetal position on the hospital bed. Rudolfo comes in with an old stuffed dog.)*

RUDOLFO: Hey Baby...

MITZI: *(not moving at all)* Hey Daddy...

RUDOLFO: Where's your mother?

MITZI: Downstairs. Buying more magazines.

RUDOLFO: Finished the Weissbaum job. Set the boys free early.

*(Mitzi nods.)*

RUDOLFO: You okay?

MITZI: My stomach's tight…

*(Pause)*

RUDOLFO: Hey. Stopped by the house and look who wanted to come.

*(Rudolfo lays the old stuffed dog next to Mitzi.)*

MITZI: Perrito.

RUDOLFO: He was pissed, man. He don't like bein' left behind.

MITZI: *(pulling the dog to her)* Thank you.

RUDOLFO: No problem.

*(Pause)*

RUDOLFO: You hear about Camie?

*(Mitzi shakes her head, no.)*

RUDOLFO: They traded him. I don't know… The M's this year…

MITZI: Yeah.

RUDOLFO: Like they had a garage sale. Just gave away their defense…

MITZI: Yeah.

RUDOLFO: *(beat)* Listen, I probably can't stay for this whole thing… you know…

MITZI: I know.

RUDOLFO: But, whatever you need, baby. You got that?

MITZI: Yeah.

*(VERA enters with magazines.)*

VERA: Okay, since we're hunkering down, I got People, Sports Illustrated, and Oprah. Magazine?

*(Lights out and then up again. A day has passed. Rudolfo is gone. Mitzi is exhausted, drugged, hunched forward, seated on the labor chair. Vera is asleep on the hospital bed with her magazines. It is very early morning.)*

MITZI: *(calling)* Nurse…?

NURSE: Yes?

MITZI: Do you think I could have another one of those shots?

NURSE: How long has it been? *(she checks her chart)*

MITZI: 6 years.

NURSE: 4 hours… I guess you're almost due.

MITZI: *(weakly)* Thank you.

NURSE: Would you like some more ice?

MITZI: No. *(she cries)*

NURSE: Oh honey… it's time to let go. You gotta let him go…

*(Mitzi dry heaves into a little plastic dish.)*

NURSE: That's the Pitocin making you sick. The doctor upped your dose. Once your body takes over and starts making your own contractions, I'll get you off that stuff… okay?

*(Mitzi nods. The Geneticist swings in for early morning rounds. This is his first stop. He carries a thick document and a pen.)*

GENETICIST: Mitzi Mendoza?

MITZI: *(raising her hand, as if in school)* Here.

GENETICIST: Ah. Oh yes. Hate to come at such a difficult time *(she heaves again)* But we're light one secretary, university budget cuts, yada-yada-yada, upshot is we didn't get your signature on the genetics profiling documentation earlier.

MITZI: *(stares at him, trying to focus)* What?

NURSE: Doctor, she's fairly anesthetized.

GENETICIST: What's she on?

NURSE: Demerol.

GENETICIST: She can sign on that. Mitzi? Take the pen.

MITZI: Who are you?

GENETICIST: I'm Dr. Davis, a geneticist on staff here at the hospital.

*(The Geneticist hands her a pen, she looks at it. Mary sneaks up from behind and attacks the Geneticist, climbing onto his back. He doesn't acknowledge this at all.)*

MITZI: You…

GENETICIST: Take the pen and I'll explain what you're signing.

*(Mitzi takes the pen, watching as Mary tries to wrestle the Geneticist down, with very little affect. Nobody else seems to notice the struggle.)*

GENETICIST: Now. These are the documents you need to sign in order for the University to do the fetal testing.

MITZI: Mom?

NURSE: *(wakes Vera up)* Mrs. Mendoza, wake up.

VERA: What? Oh hell, another bozo. *(she goes back to sleep)*

NURSE: Mrs. Mendoza, we need your help.

VERA: Sign the papers, Mitzi.

MITZI: But what are they? Tell me what they are.

GENETICIST: Why don't you read them for yourself. *(she takes the papers, squints)*

MITZI: I can't see the print.

GENETICIST: Basically these are standard forms, much like the ones you've already signed, but these are in regard to the fetal materials you're turning over to the university for testing.

VERA: What are we doing?

GENETICIST: By doing a series of genetic tests, we may be able to determine if this case of anencephaly had a genetic component to it.

VERA: Like some kind of hereditary defect? Something that can be passed on?

GENETICIST: Mitzi and her husband may want to know if they're at a higher risk for this again.

*(Mary gives up the struggle, slides down from the Geneticist. Circles him once, spitting on his shoes.)*

MITZI: What's this part?

GENETICIST: What part?

MITZI: Here.

VERA: Lemme see. *(she reads)* "Once testing is complete, all materials become the property of the University." What materials?

GENETICIST: *(beat)* Well, obviously the materials we're testing... the fetal tissues...

MITZI: You mean...? *(she snorts a laugh)* You gotta be kidding me?

VERA: Well, how much of his tissue would you take?

GENETICIST: *(beat)* I don't think you've been fully informed as to how --

MITZI: How much do you need? Like a patch or something?

NURSE: Mitzi, generally when the University agrees to do this level of testing, they're given all the tissues.

MITZI: To keep?

GENETICIST: Yes.

MITZI: Oh fuck, you mean like floating around in a jar or something?

GENETICIST: For scientific purposes.

MARY: For science, for science! Another body part for science!

MITZI:  No.

GENETICIST:  Mitzi, you need to consider this very seriously.

VERA: Sign it, Mitzi, what does it matter?

MITZI:  No.

VERA:  She means yes.  Here Doctor, just stick the paper under her hand.

MITZI:  Mom, I'm not leaving my baby with them.

VERA:  Why not?  What're you gonna do with it?

MITZI:  *(beat, looking to Mary)*  I'm gonna have a funeral.

VERA:  A what?

MITZI:  A funeral.

VERA:  That's ridiculous.  Now shape up.  You're carrying this thing too damn far.

MITZI:  I don't care what you say, I'm having a funeral for my baby.

GENETICIST:  Mitzi, need I point out, you chose to terminate your pregnancy.  Why not let it go?  Why make this any harder?

NURSE:  Doctor --

MITZI: *(sarcastic)* Chose? You mean like I got to pick one from Column A and one from Column B? Like this was a CHOICE?

MARY: It be all yer fault, you see? Oh, always, always, the woman *chose*.

GENETICIST: Take some time, think it over. I'll leave the papers right here. I guarantee, when you come back next time —-

MITZI: There's never gonna be a next time.

GENETICIST: There's always a next time. And when it comes, you'll want this information. So I'll leave these here...

VERA: I'll hang onto 'em.

MITZI: No, give them to me.

VERA: Are you gonna sign 'em and stop this nonsense?

MITZI: Give them. To me.

*(Vera hands the papers to Mitzi, who takes them and tears them up. Mary rejoices and exits. A strong contraction slowly builds and rolls over Mitzi through the following.)*

VERA: Oh that's beautiful.

GENETICIST: I'm afraid you may regret that, Mitzi.

NURSE: Doctor, can I speak with you, please...?

*(The Nurse leads the Geneticist out of the room.)*

VERA:  Well, that's just brilliant.  Baby is as baby does.

MITZI:  *(raw, in pain)*  Go home, Mama.

VERA:  What?

MITZI:  I don't want you here when he's born.  It would ruin it.  *(the pain gets greater)*  Oh God.

VERA:  Ruin it?

MITZI:  Oh my God…

VERA:  *(not yet aware of Mitzi's contraction, hurt by her rejection)*  Ohhh… I see what this is… You're lookin' to hang this all on me, just like everything else.  You don't think I know how embarrassed you are by me?

MITZI:  *(low, breathing hard, trying to stay on top of the pain)*  Mamma --

VERA:  By my mouth, the way I walk and breathe.  Don't want me at those teacher conferences, rather have Rudolfo --

MITZI:  Get the nurse!

VERA:  What – What's wrong?

MTIZI:  I think -- It hurts!

VERA:  Oh baby…!  Oh my baby, you -- you wait right there!

MITZI: *(a deep groan, her body contorts)* Ahhhhh! Oh God, Mamma!

VERA: *(calling as she exits)* Nurse! Nurse! Things are happening in here...!

*(Lights down and then up again on Mitzi. She is quiet, laying on her side in a fetal position. The process is over. Thomas Aquinas appears with a clean plastic pan.)*

AQUINAS: I come bearing gifts.

*(He hands her the pan. She takes it.)*

MITZI: Thank you.

AQUINAS: Here. *(he holds out his arm, making a muscle)* Feel my arm. Go on.

*(Mitzi feels his arm.)*

AQUINAS: Huh? Big difference?

MITZI: Yeah.

AQUINAS: Gold's Gym! I'm sold.

MITZI: *(softly)* It's over... Mr. Aquinas.

AQUINAS: Ah... Maybe I should come back another time.

MITZI: No. Don't go away.

AQUINAS: Alright... *(pondering what to do)* Would you... like to feel my other arm?

*(Mitzi shakes her head, no. Aquinas starts to pat his robes, searching.)*

AQUINAS: I believe I've got a deck of cards somewhere in here...

MITZI: *(beat)* I'm sorry, Mr. Aquinas.

AQUINAS: Whatever for?

MITZI: I don't think I can become a Catholic.

AQUINAS: Oh, my darling girl, you're talking absolute rubbish.

*(Mitzi doesn't respond)*

AQUINAS: Do you know what the One True Church exalts in? Do you know what holds the entire institution together?

*(Mitzi doesn't answer.)*

AQUINAS. Forgiveness.

MITZI: It doesn't matter.

AQUINAS: It *does* matter. Catholicism is a *living* theology, Mitzi. It breathes through the generosity of its people. We continuously redefine our truth based on the experiences and consciousness of the *sensus fidelium*, the sense of the faithful. Did you know that when my life began on Earth, the Church excommunicated people for reading Aristotle? (continued)

AQUINAS (Cont'd):   And by the time I died, they not only required scholars to read his works, but condemned as heretics anyone who argued against him. *(moving closer to her)* So, do not for one moment entertain the notion that anything that's happened in this room precludes you from the fold.   Do you understand what I'm saying to you?

*(Mitzi nods slightly.)*

AQUINAS:   You are, and always will be, loved. *(beat)* Now... when you come back to class, we can discuss all of this in greater depth...

*(Thomas Aquinas gently touches Mitzi's head, she turns away slightly.)*

AQUINAS:   Goodbye, Mitzi.

MITZI:   Goodbye.

*(Aquinas walks out of the light.   A table is pushed toward Mitzi.   She and Chuck now sit uncomfortably at a restaurant.   Mitzi has a small, square cardboard box with her. While she says the following, she avoids looking directly at Chuck.)*

MITZI:   And... at some point... before everything gets rolling, somebody gives you this little book.   I can't remember who... maybe the social worker.   But, it's this book about termination and stillbirth, right? Called 'When Hello Means Goodbye'.   And inside, they give you all this like practical advice, about what to do when you know you're going to deliver a dead baby.      (continued)

MITZI (Cont'd):  They suggest that you name the baby. That you… look at him, you know?  When he comes out.  Which sounds so awful and gross, because based on his problems, you're imagining this horrible monster.  So, at first, these things seem really sick to you. Or at least they did to me...  They even tell you to hold him, and photograph him, and you think, oh my God, these people are nuts!  I mean how disgusting… *(beat)*  But… then he finally comes.  And you can't help it… you're like drawn to his face, his quiet, bruised little body.  And he doesn't look hideous at all, just… really, really tired.  And there are even certain family features that you recognize.  And he's got these perfect little feet and hands.  And suddenly, you are just… so happy!  About the sheer, like, REALness of these appendages.  You know?  They exist!  They have been alive.  And they opened and closed up into tiny little fists, and beat on you from the inside, as if saying 'hurry up and check me out, I won't be around for long'.  And it just feels really good to know that you have not made this little guy up.  That he was real. And… even though… I can already see he's fading from my family and friends, and stuff… I don't think he's ever gonna fade for me, you know?  Because no one else ever felt him, knew him when he lived.  Only me.  Only me, you know Chuck…?

*(Mitzi finally looks at Chuck.)*

MITZI:  *(offering the square box to Chuck)*  Here.  I had him cremated.  I haven't had the funeral yet.  I wasn't sure if you'd want half the ashes… or what.

CHUCK:  *(thoroughly uncomfortable)*  No, hey.  That's. Let's just keep it all together.

MITZI: Okay. *(offering the box again)* But feel it. It's heavier than you'd think. I mean, being that he was such a small guy. Oh. And Chuck... *(she opens the box)* You gotta see these... they're his molars. Like little white stars, in all this dust. I guess they don't burn --

CHUCK: No! Fuck. Jesus, Mitzi, what's the matter with you? I mean are you fucking nuts or something?

*(Pause)*

MITZI: I just thought... if you saw them... maybe it would make him more real for you.

CHUCK: I don't want him more real, so put that the fuck away.

*(Pause. Mitzi closes up the box. Long silence. Chuck regrets his last outburst, approaches the next part as gently as he's able.)*

CHUCK: I've been transferred to North Carolina. Hospital Supplies.

MITZI: Yeah. I heard. *(beat)* When do you...?

CHUCK: Pretty much right away. I've already packed up my stuff from the apartment. *(beat)* The yellow looks good.

MITZI: Thanks.

*(Pause)*

CHUCK: So…

*(Pause)*

CHUCK: You could come later, maybe…

MITZI: Yeah…

CHUCK: Meet me…

MITZI: *(beat)* Sure. *(beat)* Whatever.

*(Neither one seems really interested in this. Chuck nods. Not sure what else to say, he carefully lays down money for the check, looks at Mitzi one last time, and leaves. Lights up on Reckless Mary, vibrating in the Sharper Image chair. Aquinas stands with his arms crossed, watching her.)*

MARY: Ohhhhhhh, your Flatulence, where've you been hiding this contraption?

AQUINAS: That's my chair, witch.

MARY: Now *this* be truly the devil's handiwork.

AQUINAS: You have no rights to it. Get out.

MARY: Buzz off.

AQUINAS: I am asking you nicely to vacant the chair.

MARY: Not a chance in Hell.

AQUINAS: Why you knock-kneed Daughter of Baal…

MARY: Sticks and stones may break my –

AQUINAS: *(this is a roar)* GET OUT OF MY CHAIR!!!

*(Pause. Mary doesn't move.)*

MARY: No.

AQUINAS: No? What do you mean, no?

MARY: The winds have changed, curate. This chair will never belong solely to Your Wordiness again. Use your precious Faith and Reason to fathom that!

AQUINAS: Heretic!

MARY: The sting be gone from that bit a name-calling I'm afraid. No, Aquinas, I shall lay like a leech on this chair and not rise again for love nor money.

*(Aquinas ponders this, gives in)*

AQUINAS: Alright. You leave me no choice…

*(Aquinas turns slowly around and aims his gargantuan rear towards the chair.)*

AQUINAS: Clear!

MARY: Wait, you imbecile, there be no room!

*(Aquinas sits with a thud. They are now wedged, side-by-side, in the chair.)*

MARY:  Bloody whale, you made me drop the controls.

*(Aquinas fishes below him for the string that's attached to the controls, he reels it in, and hands it to Mary.)*

AQUINAS:  Here…

MARY:  Thank you.

AQUINAS:  Turn it up.

MARY:  How high?

AQUINAS:  Eight or nine.

*(Mary does as commanded, the chair is noticeably louder.)*

MARY:  Oh yes!

AQUINAS:  Heaven.

MARY AND AQUINAS:  *(with vibrato)*  Ahhhhhhhh…

*(Lights down on Mary and Aquinas, and up on Mitzi, with Vera, Rudolfo, and Nita, each holding a daffodil, standing by the shoreline at Lincoln Park.  Tim walks up and joins the group, Nita hands him a daffodil.)*

MITZI:  *(finishing up her service)*  So… I guess, that's all. I guess… I just wanted a chance to say goodbye to you, you know Henry?  Thank you for… for being. I'm just, I'm glad you were here. *(to everyone)*  Okay. Umm. Let's pray…

NITA: You mean, like, *pray*?

MITZI: Yeah.

*(The three women bow their heads. Rudolfo moves closer to Tim, in the back.)*

RUDOLFO: You know, all this… *(indicating everything that's happened)* This is not the place for a man to go sticking his nose in.

TIM: Boy, howdy.

RUDOLFO: I mean, that's my own personal opinion, you know. Used to be, the woman took care of the 'woman-things'. Men just heard about it later, after the fact. When it came to woman-things, my mother never asked my father nothin, you know? She didn't want to upset him, cause him emotional pain. She took the pain. When she found herself pregnant 3 months after my brother was born and my father'd been laid off in the orchards, she didn't say nada. She just 'went to her sister's in Portland'. Came back re-lieved. I think she 'went to her sister's' twice. Everybody did. Nobody put it in the papers. It was private business. Woman business.

TIM: Gotcha.

*(Mitzi raises her head.)*

MITZI: Okay.

VERA: *(to Mitzi, gently)* Was that it?

MITZI: Yeah. You think I need more?

VERA: No, it sounded real good. Should we throw in our daffodils now?

MITZI: *(beat)* Yeah. Throw 'em in…

*(One-by-one they each toss their daffodil into the water. Mitzi stands slightly forward of the others, searching for one last gesture to give to her son. She starts to sing 'Somewhere Over the Rainbow' a cappella, in Esperanto.)*

MITZI: IE SUPER LA ARKO
      DE L'CIEL'
      KUSAS LANDO MIRINDA
      DIRAS AL NI FABEL'.
      IE SUPER LA ARKO…

*(Mitzi can't remember the next line. Nita gently gives it to her.)*

NITA: EN LA BLU'

MITZI: EN LA BLU'

*(Mitzi finishes the song herself.)*

MITZI: REVOJ IGAS REALAJ
      REGAS SENZORGA GU'.

*(Lights out. End of play.)*

# NOTES

# NOTES

# Original Works

www.originalworksonline.com

Made in the USA
Middletown, DE
16 October 2020